MW00929869

>>>———————————————————<<<

THIS BOOK BELONGS TO

>>>———————————————————<<<

DATE

TIME

LOCATION

WEATHER CONDITIONS

HUNTING TYPE

CO-HUNTERS

TERRAIN LEVEL

EASY 1 2 3 4 5 HARD

GEAR / SET UP

TARGET AREA

♂

♀

AMMUNITION

ACTIVITY & SIGHTINGS

TYPES OF FLORA

ADDITIONAL NOTES

DATE

TIME

LOCATION

WEATHER CONDITIONS

☀ ⛅ ☁ 🌧 ❄

HUNTING TYPE

CO-HUNTERS

TERRAIN LEVEL

| | 1 | 2 | 3 | 4 | 5 | |
| EASY | ○ | ○ | ○ | ○ | ○ | HARD |

GEAR / SET UP

AMMUNITION

TARGET AREA

♂
☐

♀
☐

ACTIVITY & SIGHTINGS

TYPES OF FLORA

ADDITIONAL NOTES

📅 DATE		**WEATHER CONDITIONS**

DATE

TIME

LOCATION

WEATHER CONDITIONS

🌡 —— ☀ ⛅ 🌧 ⛈ ❄

🚩 —— ☐ ☐ ☐ ☐ ☐

HUNTING TYPE

CO-HUNTERS

TERRAIN LEVEL

🌳 1   2   3   4   5 🏔
EASY ◯ ——◯——◯——◯—— ◯ HARD

GEAR / SET UP

TARGET AREA

♂
☐

♀
☐

AMMUNITION

ACTIVITY & SIGHTINGS

TYPES OF FLORA

ADDITIONAL NOTES

DATE

TIME

LOCATION

HUNTING TYPE

CO-HUNTERS

WEATHER CONDITIONS

TERRAIN LEVEL

1   2   3   4   5

EASY   HARD

GEAR / SET UP

AMMUNITION

TARGET AREA

♂

♀

ACTIVITY & SIGHTINGS

TYPES OF FLORA

ADDITIONAL NOTES

DATE

TIME

LOCATION

WEATHER CONDITIONS

HUNTING TYPE

CO-HUNTERS

TERRAIN LEVEL

EASY 1 2 3 4 5 HARD

GEAR / SET UP

TARGET AREA

♂

♀

AMMUNITION

ACTIVITY & SIGHTINGS

TYPES OF FLORA

ADDITIONAL NOTES

DATE

TIME

LOCATION

WEATHER CONDITIONS

HUNTING TYPE

CO-HUNTERS

TERRAIN LEVEL

1   2   3   4   5

EASY   HARD

GEAR / SET UP

AMMUNITION

TARGET AREA

♂

♀

ACTIVITY & SIGHTINGS

TYPES OF FLORA

ADDITIONAL NOTES

DATE

TIME

LOCATION

WEATHER CONDITIONS

HUNTING TYPE

CO-HUNTERS

TERRAIN LEVEL

EASY 1   2   3   4   5 HA...

GEAR / SET UP

TARGET AREA

♂

♀

AMMUNITION

ACTIVITY & SIGHTINGS

TYPES OF FLORA

ADDITIONAL NOTES

DATE

TIME

LOCATION

HUNTING TYPE

CO-HUNTERS

WEATHER CONDITIONS

TERRAIN LEVEL

	1	2	3	4	5	
EASY	○	○	○	○	○	HARD

GEAR / SET UP

AMMUNITION

TARGET AREA

♂

♀

ACTIVITY & SIGHTINGS

TYPES OF FLORA

ADDITIONAL NOTES

DATE

TIME

LOCATION

WEATHER CONDITIONS

HUNTING TYPE

CO-HUNTERS

TERRAIN LEVEL

1   2   3   4   5

EASY   HARD

GEAR / SET UP

TARGET AREA

♂

♀

AMMUNITION

ACTIVITY & SIGHTINGS

TYPES OF FLORA

ADDITIONAL NOTES

DATE

TIME

LOCATION

HUNTING TYPE

CO-HUNTERS

WEATHER CONDITIONS

TERRAIN LEVEL

	1	2	3	4	5	
EASY	○	○	○	○	○	HARD

GEAR / SET UP

AMMUNITION

TARGET AREA

♂

♀

ACTIVITY & SIGHTINGS

TYPES OF FLORA

ADDITIONAL NOTES

DATE

TIME

LOCATION

WEATHER CONDITIONS

HUNTING TYPE

CO-HUNTERS

TERRAIN LEVEL

EASY 1 2 3 4 5 HARD

GEAR / SET UP

TARGET AREA

♂
☐

♀
☐

AMMUNITION

ACTIVITY & SIGHTINGS

TYPES OF FLORA

ADDITIONAL NOTES

DATE

TIME

LOCATION

WEATHER CONDITIONS

HUNTING TYPE

CO-HUNTERS

TERRAIN LEVEL

EASY 1   2   3   4   5 HARD

GEAR / SET UP

TARGET AREA

♂

♀

AMMUNITION

ACTIVITY & SIGHTINGS

TYPES OF FLORA

ADDITIONAL NOTES

DATE	WEATHER CONDITIONS

DATE

TIME

LOCATION

WEATHER CONDITIONS

☀ ⛅ ☁ 🌧 ❄

☐ ☐ ☐ ☐ ☐

HUNTING TYPE

CO-HUNTERS

TERRAIN LEVEL

	1	2	3	4	5	
EASY	○	○	○	○	○	HA

GEAR / SET UP

TARGET AREA

♂
☐

♀
☐

AMMUNITION

ACTIVITY & SIGHTINGS

TYPES OF FLORA

ADDITIONAL NOTES

DATE

TIME

LOCATION

WEATHER CONDITIONS

HUNTING TYPE

CO-HUNTERS

TERRAIN LEVEL

EASY 1 2 3 4 5 HARD

GEAR / SET UP

TARGET AREA

♂

♀

AMMUNITION

ACTIVITY & SIGHTINGS

TYPES OF FLORA

ADDITIONAL NOTES

DATE

TIME

LOCATION

WEATHER CONDITIONS

HUNTING TYPE

CO-HUNTERS

TERRAIN LEVEL

1   2   3   4   5

EASY   HARD

GEAR / SET UP

TARGET AREA

$\male$

$\female$

AMMUNITION

ACTIVITY & SIGHTINGS

TYPES OF FLORA

ADDITIONAL NOTES

DATE

TIME

LOCATION

HUNTING TYPE

CO-HUNTERS

WEATHER CONDITIONS

TERRAIN LEVEL

1   2   3   4   5

EASY   HARD

GEAR / SET UP

AMMUNITION

TARGET AREA

♂

♀

ACTIVITY & SIGHTINGS

TYPES OF FLORA

ADDITIONAL NOTES

DATE

TIME

LOCATION

WEATHER CONDITIONS

HUNTING TYPE

CO-HUNTERS

TERRAIN LEVEL

EASY 1 2 3 4 5 HARD

GEAR / SET UP

TARGET AREA

♂

♀

AMMUNITION

ACTIVITY & SIGHTINGS

TYPES OF FLORA

ADDITIONAL NOTES

DATE

TIME

LOCATION

WEATHER CONDITIONS

HUNTING TYPE

CO-HUNTERS

TERRAIN LEVEL

1   2   3   4   5

EASY   HARD

GEAR / SET UP

AMMUNITION

TARGET AREA

♂

♀

ACTIVITY & SIGHTINGS

TYPES OF FLORA

ADDITIONAL NOTES

DATE

TIME

LOCATION

WEATHER CONDITIONS

HUNTING TYPE

CO-HUNTERS

TERRAIN LEVEL

EASY 1 2 3 4 5 HA

GEAR / SET UP

TARGET AREA

AMMUNITION

ACTIVITY & SIGHTINGS

TYPES OF FLORA

ADDITIONAL NOTES

DATE

TIME

LOCATION

WEATHER CONDITIONS

☼ ⛅ 🌧 ⛈ ❄
☐ ☐ ☐ ☐ ☐

HUNTING TYPE

CO-HUNTERS

TERRAIN LEVEL

EASY 1 — 2 — 3 — 4 — 5 HARD
○ ○ ○ ○ ○

GEAR / SET UP

TARGET AREA

♂
☐

♀
☐

AMMUNITION

ACTIVITY & SIGHTINGS

TYPES OF FLORA

ADDITIONAL NOTES

DATE

TIME

LOCATION

WEATHER CONDITIONS

HUNTING TYPE

CO-HUNTERS

TERRAIN LEVEL

1	2	3	4	5
EASY				HARD

GEAR / SET UP

TARGET AREA

♂

♀

AMMUNITION

ACTIVITY & SIGHTINGS

TYPES OF FLORA

ADDITIONAL NOTES

DATE

TIME

LOCATION

WEATHER CONDITIONS

HUNTING TYPE

CO-HUNTERS

TERRAIN LEVEL

1　　2　　3　　4　　5

EASY　　　　　　　　　　HARD

GEAR / SET UP

TARGET AREA

♂

♀

AMMUNITION

ACTIVITY & SIGHTINGS

TYPES OF FLORA

ADDITIONAL NOTES

DATE

TIME

LOCATION

WEATHER CONDITIONS

HUNTING TYPE

CO-HUNTERS

TERRAIN LEVEL

1 2 3 4 5

EASY HARD

GEAR / SET UP

AMMUNITION

TARGET AREA

♂

♀

ACTIVITY & SIGHTINGS

TYPES OF FLORA

ADDITIONAL NOTES

DATE

TIME

LOCATION

WEATHER CONDITIONS

HUNTING TYPE

CO-HUNTERS

TERRAIN LEVEL

EASY 1 2 3 4 5 HARD

GEAR / SET UP

TARGET AREA

♂

♀

AMMUNITION

ACTIVITY & SIGHTINGS

TYPES OF FLORA

ADDITIONAL NOTES

DATE

TIME

LOCATION

WEATHER CONDITIONS

HUNTING TYPE

CO-HUNTERS

TERRAIN LEVEL

EASY 1 2 3 4 5 HA[RD]

GEAR / SET UP

AMMUNITION

TARGET AREA

♂
♀

ACTIVITY & SIGHTINGS

TYPES OF FLORA

ADDITIONAL NOTES

DATE

TIME

LOCATION

HUNTING TYPE

CO-HUNTERS

WEATHER CONDITIONS

TERRAIN LEVEL

EASY 1 2 3 4 5 HARD

GEAR / SET UP

TARGET AREA

♂

♀

AMMUNITION

ACTIVITY & SIGHTINGS

TYPES OF FLORA

ADDITIONAL NOTES

DATE

TIME

LOCATION

WEATHER CONDITIONS

HUNTING TYPE

CO-HUNTERS

TERRAIN LEVEL

EASY 1 2 3 4 5 HARD

GEAR / SET UP

TARGET AREA

♂
☐

♀
☐

AMMUNITION

ACTIVITY & SIGHTINGS

TYPES OF FLORA

ADDITIONAL NOTES

DATE

TIME

LOCATION

HUNTING TYPE

CO-HUNTERS

WEATHER CONDITIONS

TERRAIN LEVEL

EASY 1 2 3 4 5 HARD

GEAR / SET UP

AMMUNITION

TARGET AREA

♂
☐

♀
☐

ACTIVITY & SIGHTINGS

TYPES OF FLORA

ADDITIONAL NOTES

DATE

TIME

LOCATION

WEATHER CONDITIONS

HUNTING TYPE

CO-HUNTERS

TERRAIN LEVEL

EASY 1 2 3 4 5 HARD

GEAR / SET UP

TARGET AREA

♂

♀

AMMUNITION

ACTIVITY & SIGHTINGS

TYPES OF FLORA

ADDITIONAL NOTES

DATE

TIME

LOCATION

WEATHER CONDITIONS

HUNTING TYPE

CO-HUNTERS

TERRAIN LEVEL

EASY 1   2   3   4   5 HARD

GEAR / SET UP

TARGET AREA

♂

♀

AMMUNITION

ACTIVITY & SIGHTINGS

TYPES OF FLORA

ADDITIONAL NOTES

DATE

TIME

LOCATION

WEATHER CONDITIONS

🌡 —— ☀ ⛅ 🌧 ⛈ ❄

🚩 —— ☐ ☐ ☐ ☐ ☐

HUNTING TYPE

CO-HUNTERS

TERRAIN LEVEL

	1	2	3	4	5	
EASY	○	○	○	○	○	HA

GEAR / SET UP

AMMUNITION

TARGET AREA

♂
☐

♀
☐

ACTIVITY & SIGHTINGS

TYPES OF FLORA

ADDITIONAL NOTES

DATE

TIME

LOCATION

HUNTING TYPE

CO-HUNTERS

WEATHER CONDITIONS

TERRAIN LEVEL

EASY 1 2 3 4 5 HARD

GEAR / SET UP

AMMUNITION

TARGET AREA

♂

♀

ACTIVITY & SIGHTINGS

TYPES OF FLORA

ADDITIONAL NOTES

📅 **DATE**

🕐 **TIME**

📍 **LOCATION**

WEATHER CONDITIONS

🌡 ___ ☀ ⛅ 🌧 ⛈ ❄

🚩 ___ ☐ ☐ ☐ ☐ ☐

⊕ **HUNTING TYPE**

👤 **CO-HUNTERS**

TERRAIN LEVEL

🌳   1   2   3   4   5   🏔

EASY ◯   ◯   ◯   ◯   ◯   HARD

GEAR / SET UP

TARGET AREA

♂ ☐

♀ ☐

AMMUNITION

ACTIVITY & SIGHTINGS

TYPES OF FLORA

ADDITIONAL NOTES

DATE

TIME

LOCATION

WEATHER CONDITIONS

HUNTING TYPE

CO-HUNTERS

TERRAIN LEVEL

1   2   3   4   5

EASY   HARD

GEAR / SET UP

AMMUNITION

TARGET AREA

♂

♀

ACTIVITY & SIGHTINGS

TYPES OF FLORA

ADDITIONAL NOTES

DATE

TIME

LOCATION

WEATHER CONDITIONS

🌡 ____ ☀ ⛅ 🌧 ⛈ ❄

🚩 ____ ☐ ☐ ☐ ☐ ☐

HUNTING TYPE

CO-HUNTERS

TERRAIN LEVEL

	1	2	3	4	5	
EASY	○	○	○	○	○	HAR

GEAR / SET UP

TARGET AREA

♂
☐

♀
☐

AMMUNITION

ACTIVITY & SIGHTINGS

TYPES OF FLORA

ADDITIONAL NOTES

DATE

TIME

LOCATION

WEATHER CONDITIONS

HUNTING TYPE

CO-HUNTERS

TERRAIN LEVEL

1   2   3   4   5

EASY   HARD

GEAR / SET UP

AMMUNITION

TARGET AREA

♂

♀

ACTIVITY & SIGHTINGS

TYPES OF FLORA

ADDITIONAL NOTES

DATE

TIME

LOCATION

WEATHER CONDITIONS

HUNTING TYPE

CO-HUNTERS

TERRAIN LEVEL

EASY 1 2 3 4 5 HA

GEAR / SET UP

AMMUNITION

TARGET AREA

♂

♀

ACTIVITY & SIGHTINGS

TYPES OF FLORA

ADDITIONAL NOTES

DATE

TIME

LOCATION

WEATHER CONDITIONS

HUNTING TYPE

CO-HUNTERS

TERRAIN LEVEL

	1	2	3	4	5	
EASY	◯	◯	◯	◯	◯	HARD

GEAR / SET UP

AMMUNITION

TARGET AREA

♂
☐

♀
☐

ACTIVITY & SIGHTINGS

TYPES OF FLORA

ADDITIONAL NOTES

DATE

TIME

LOCATION

WEATHER CONDITIONS

HUNTING TYPE

CO-HUNTERS

TERRAIN LEVEL

EASY 1 2 3 4 5 HARD

GEAR / SET UP

AMMUNITION

TARGET AREA

♂

♀

ACTIVITY & SIGHTINGS

TYPES OF FLORA

ADDITIONAL NOTES

DATE

TIME

LOCATION

HUNTING TYPE

CO-HUNTERS

WEATHER CONDITIONS

☐ ☐ ☐ ☐ ☐

TERRAIN LEVEL

1   2   3   4   5

EASY ○   ○   ○   ○   ○ HARD

GEAR / SET UP

AMMUNITION

TARGET AREA

♂
☐

♀
☐

ACTIVITY & SIGHTINGS

TYPES OF FLORA

ADDITIONAL NOTES

DATE		WEATHER CONDITIONS

DATE

TIME

LOCATION

WEATHER CONDITIONS

☀ ⛅ ☁ ⛈ ❄

HUNTING TYPE

CO-HUNTERS

TERRAIN LEVEL

EASY ○ 1 ○ 2 ○ 3 ○ 4 ○ 5 HAR

GEAR / SET UP

TARGET AREA

♂
☐

♀
☐

AMMUNITION

ACTIVITY & SIGHTINGS

TYPES OF FLORA

ADDITIONAL NOTES

DATE

TIME

LOCATION

WEATHER CONDITIONS

HUNTING TYPE

CO-HUNTERS

TERRAIN LEVEL

EASY 1 2 3 4 5 HARD

GEAR / SET UP

TARGET AREA

♂

♀

AMMUNITION

ACTIVITY & SIGHTINGS

TYPES OF FLORA

ADDITIONAL NOTES

DATE

TIME

LOCATION

WEATHER CONDITIONS

🌡 ___ ☀ ⛅ 🌧 ⛈ ❄

🏳 ___ ☐ ☐ ☐ ☐ ☐

HUNTING TYPE

CO-HUNTERS

TERRAIN LEVEL

	1	2	3	4	5	
EASY	○	○	○	○	○	HA

GEAR / SET UP

AMMUNITION

TARGET AREA

♂
☐

♀
☐

ACTIVITY & SIGHTINGS

TYPES OF FLORA

ADDITIONAL NOTES

DATE

TIME

LOCATION

WEATHER CONDITIONS

HUNTING TYPE

CO-HUNTERS

TERRAIN LEVEL

1	2	3	4	5

EASY ○ ○ ○ ○ ○ HARD

GEAR / SET UP

AMMUNITION

TARGET AREA

♂
☐

♀
☐

ACTIVITY & SIGHTINGS

TYPES OF FLORA

ADDITIONAL NOTES

DATE

TIME

LOCATION

WEATHER CONDITIONS

🌡 ___   ☀ ⛅ 🌧 ⛈ ❄

🏳 ___   ☐ ☐ ☐ ☐ ☐

HUNTING TYPE

CO-HUNTERS

TERRAIN LEVEL

EASY   1   2   3   4   5   HARD
       ○   ○   ○   ○   ○

GEAR / SET UP

TARGET AREA

♂
☐

♀
☐

AMMUNITION

ACTIVITY & SIGHTINGS

TYPES OF FLORA

ADDITIONAL NOTES

DATE

TIME

LOCATION

WEATHER CONDITIONS

☀ ⛅ 🌧 ⛈ ❄

☐ ☐ ☐ ☐ ☐

HUNTING TYPE

CO-HUNTERS

TERRAIN LEVEL

	1	2	3	4	5	
EASY	○	○	○	○	○	HARD

GEAR / SET UP

TARGET AREA

♂
☐

♀
☐

AMMUNITION

ACTIVITY & SIGHTINGS

TYPES OF FLORA

ADDITIONAL NOTES

DATE

TIME

LOCATION

WEATHER CONDITIONS

HUNTING TYPE

CO-HUNTERS

TERRAIN LEVEL

EASY 1   2   3   4   5 HAR

GEAR / SET UP

TARGET AREA

♂
☐

♀
☐

AMMUNITION

ACTIVITY & SIGHTINGS

TYPES OF FLORA

ADDITIONAL NOTES

DATE

TIME

LOCATION

WEATHER CONDITIONS

HUNTING TYPE

CO-HUNTERS

TERRAIN LEVEL

1   2   3   4   5

EASY   HARD

GEAR / SET UP

AMMUNITION

TARGET AREA

♂

♀

ACTIVITY & SIGHTINGS

TYPES OF FLORA

ADDITIONAL NOTES

DATE	WEATHER CONDITIONS

TIME	

LOCATION	

HUNTING TYPE

CO-HUNTERS

TERRAIN LEVEL

1 2 3 4 5

EASY HARD

GEAR / SET UP

TARGET AREA

♂

♀

AMMUNITION

ACTIVITY & SIGHTINGS

TYPES OF FLORA

ADDITIONAL NOTES

DATE

TIME

LOCATION

WEATHER CONDITIONS

HUNTING TYPE

CO-HUNTERS

TERRAIN LEVEL

1   2   3   4   5

EASY   HARD

GEAR / SET UP

AMMUNITION

TARGET AREA

♂

♀

ACTIVITY & SIGHTINGS

TYPES OF FLORA

ADDITIONAL NOTES

DATE

TIME

LOCATION

WEATHER CONDITIONS

HUNTING TYPE

CO-HUNTERS

TERRAIN LEVEL

EASY 1 2 3 4 5 HARD

GEAR / SET UP

TARGET AREA

♂
☐

♀
☐

AMMUNITION

ACTIVITY & SIGHTINGS

TYPES OF FLORA

ADDITIONAL NOTES

DATE

TIME

LOCATION

HUNTING TYPE

CO-HUNTERS

WEATHER CONDITIONS

☀ ⛅ 🌧 ⛈ ❄

☐ ☐ ☐ ☐ ☐

TERRAIN LEVEL

| 1 | 2 | 3 | 4 | 5 |

EASY ○ ○ ○ ○ ○ HARD

GEAR / SET UP

AMMUNITION

TARGET AREA

♂
☐

♀
☐

ACTIVITY & SIGHTINGS

TYPES OF FLORA

ADDITIONAL NOTES

DATE

TIME

LOCATION

WEATHER CONDITIONS

🌡 —   ☀ ⛅ 🌧 ⛈ ❄

🚩 —   ☐ ☐ ☐ ☐ ☐

HUNTING TYPE

CO-HUNTERS

TERRAIN LEVEL

EASY   1   2   3   4   5   HAR

GEAR / SET UP

TARGET AREA

♂
☐

♀
☐

AMMUNITION

ACTIVITY & SIGHTINGS

TYPES OF FLORA

ADDITIONAL NOTES

DATE

TIME

LOCATION

WEATHER CONDITIONS

HUNTING TYPE

CO-HUNTERS

TERRAIN LEVEL

1   2   3   4   5

EASY ○ ○ ○ ○ ○ HARD

GEAR / SET UP

AMMUNITION

TARGET AREA

♂ ☐

♀ ☐

ACTIVITY & SIGHTINGS

TYPES OF FLORA

ADDITIONAL NOTES

DATE

TIME

LOCATION

WEATHER CONDITIONS

🌡 — ☀ ⛅ 🌧 ⛈ ❄

🚩 — ☐ ☐ ☐ ☐ ☐

HUNTING TYPE

CO-HUNTERS

TERRAIN LEVEL

EASY 1 2 3 4 5 HA
○ ○ ○ ○ ○

GEAR / SET UP

AMMUNITION

TARGET AREA

♂
☐

♀
☐

ACTIVITY & SIGHTINGS

TYPES OF FLORA

ADDITIONAL NOTES

DATE

TIME

LOCATION

WEATHER CONDITIONS

HUNTING TYPE

CO-HUNTERS

TERRAIN LEVEL

	1	2	3	4	5	
EASY	○	○	○	○	○	HARD

GEAR / SET UP

TARGET AREA

♂

♀

AMMUNITION

ACTIVITY & SIGHTINGS

TYPES OF FLORA

ADDITIONAL NOTES

DATE

TIME

LOCATION

WEATHER CONDITIONS

HUNTING TYPE

CO-HUNTERS

TERRAIN LEVEL

1   2   3   4   5

EASY   HARD

GEAR / SET UP

TARGET AREA

♂
☐

♀
☐

AMMUNITION

ACTIVITY & SIGHTINGS

TYPES OF FLORA

ADDITIONAL NOTES

DATE

TIME

LOCATION

WEATHER CONDITIONS

HUNTING TYPE

CO-HUNTERS

TERRAIN LEVEL

EASY 1 2 3 4 5 HARD

GEAR / SET UP

TARGET AREA

♂

♀

AMMUNITION

ACTIVITY & SIGHTINGS

TYPES OF FLORA

ADDITIONAL NOTES

DATE

TIME

LOCATION

WEATHER CONDITIONS

🌡 ____ ☀ ⛅ 🌧 ⛈ ❄

🚩 ____ ☐ ☐ ☐ ☐ ☐

HUNTING TYPE

CO-HUNTERS

TERRAIN LEVEL

EASY 1 2 3 4 5 HARD
○ ○ ○ ○ ○

GEAR / SET UP

AMMUNITION

TARGET AREA

♂ ☐

♀ ☐

ACTIVITY & SIGHTINGS

TYPES OF FLORA

ADDITIONAL NOTES

DATE

TIME

LOCATION

WEATHER CONDITIONS

🌡 — ☀ ⛅ 🌧 ⛈ ❄

🚩 — ☐ ☐ ☐ ☐ ☐

HUNTING TYPE

CO-HUNTERS

TERRAIN LEVEL

| | 1 | 2 | 3 | 4 | 5 | |
EASY ◯ ◯ ◯ ◯ ◯ HARD

GEAR / SET UP

AMMUNITION

TARGET AREA

♂ ☐

♀ ☐

ACTIVITY & SIGHTINGS

TYPES OF FLORA

ADDITIONAL NOTES

DATE		WEATHER CONDITIONS

DATE

TIME

LOCATION

WEATHER CONDITIONS

🌡 — ☀ ⛅ ☁ 🌧 ❄

🚩 — ☐ ☐ ☐ ☐ ☐

HUNTING TYPE

CO-HUNTERS

TERRAIN LEVEL

🌲 1   2   3   4   5 ☀
EASY ○   ○   ○   ○   ○ HA

GEAR / SET UP

TARGET AREA

♂
☐

♀
☐

AMMUNITION

ACTIVITY & SIGHTINGS

TYPES OF FLORA

ADDITIONAL NOTES

DATE

TIME

LOCATION

WEATHER CONDITIONS

HUNTING TYPE

CO-HUNTERS

TERRAIN LEVEL

EASY 1 2 3 4 5 HARD

GEAR / SET UP

TARGET AREA

♂

♀

AMMUNITION

ACTIVITY & SIGHTINGS

TYPES OF FLORA

ADDITIONAL NOTES

DATE

TIME

LOCATION

WEATHER CONDITIONS

HUNTING TYPE

CO-HUNTERS

TERRAIN LEVEL

EASY 1 2 3 4 5 HARD

GEAR / SET UP

TARGET AREA

♂

♀

AMMUNITION

ACTIVITY & SIGHTINGS

TYPES OF FLORA

ADDITIONAL NOTES

DATE

TIME

LOCATION

WEATHER CONDITIONS

HUNTING TYPE

CO-HUNTERS

TERRAIN LEVEL

EASY 1 2 3 4 5 HARD

GEAR / SET UP

AMMUNITION

TARGET AREA

♂

♀

ACTIVITY & SIGHTINGS

TYPES OF FLORA

ADDITIONAL NOTES

DATE

TIME

LOCATION

WEATHER CONDITIONS

HUNTING TYPE

CO-HUNTERS

TERRAIN LEVEL

EASY 1 2 3 4 5 HARD

GEAR / SET UP

TARGET AREA

♂
☐

♀
☐

AMMUNITION

ACTIVITY & SIGHTINGS

TYPES OF FLORA

ADDITIONAL NOTES

DATE

TIME

LOCATION

WEATHER CONDITIONS

HUNTING TYPE

CO-HUNTERS

TERRAIN LEVEL

1   2   3   4   5

EASY   HARD

GEAR / SET UP

TARGET AREA

♂

♀

AMMUNITION

ACTIVITY & SIGHTINGS

TYPES OF FLORA

ADDITIONAL NOTES

DATE

TIME

LOCATION

WEATHER CONDITIONS

HUNTING TYPE

CO-HUNTERS

TERRAIN LEVEL

EASY   1   2   3   4   5   HA...

GEAR / SET UP

TARGET AREA

♂

♀

AMMUNITION

ACTIVITY & SIGHTINGS

TYPES OF FLORA

ADDITIONAL NOTES

DATE

TIME

LOCATION

WEATHER CONDITIONS

🌡 —— ☀ ⛅ 🌧 ⛈ ❄
🚩 —— ☐ ☐ ☐ ☐ ☐

HUNTING TYPE

CO-HUNTERS

TERRAIN LEVEL

EASY 1 2 3 4 5 HARD

GEAR / SET UP

AMMUNITION

TARGET AREA

♂ ☐

♀ ☐

ACTIVITY & SIGHTINGS

TYPES OF FLORA

ADDITIONAL NOTES

DATE

TIME

LOCATION

WEATHER CONDITIONS

🌡 —— ☀ ⛅ 🌦 🌧 ❄

🎐 —— ☐ ☐ ☐ ☐ ☐

HUNTING TYPE

CO-HUNTERS

TERRAIN LEVEL

EASY 1 ○ 2 ○ 3 ○ 4 ○ 5 ○ HARD

GEAR / SET UP

AMMUNITION

TARGET AREA

♂ ☐

♀ ☐

ACTIVITY & SIGHTINGS

TYPES OF FLORA

ADDITIONAL NOTES

DATE

TIME

LOCATION

HUNTING TYPE

CO-HUNTERS

WEATHER CONDITIONS

TERRAIN LEVEL

1 2 3 4 5

EASY ○ ○ ○ ○ ○ HARD

GEAR / SET UP

AMMUNITION

ACTIVITY & SIGHTINGS

TARGET AREA

♂
☐

♀
☐

TYPES OF FLORA

ADDITIONAL NOTES

DATE

TIME

LOCATION

WEATHER CONDITIONS

☀ ⛅ ☁ ⛈ ❄

☐ ☐ ☐ ☐ ☐

HUNTING TYPE

CO-HUNTERS

TERRAIN LEVEL

EASY 1 2 3 4 5 HARD

GEAR / SET UP

AMMUNITION

TARGET AREA

♂
☐

♀
☐

ACTIVITY & SIGHTINGS

TYPES OF FLORA

ADDITIONAL NOTES

DATE

TIME

LOCATION

WEATHER CONDITIONS

☀ ⛅ ☁ 🌧 ❄

☐ ☐ ☐ ☐ ☐

HUNTING TYPE

CO-HUNTERS

TERRAIN LEVEL

EASY 1 2 3 4 5 HARD

○ ○ ○ ○ ○

GEAR / SET UP

AMMUNITION

TARGET AREA

♂ ☐

♀ ☐

ACTIVITY & SIGHTINGS

TYPES OF FLORA

ADDITIONAL NOTES

DATE

TIME

LOCATION

WEATHER CONDITIONS

HUNTING TYPE

CO-HUNTERS

TERRAIN LEVEL

EASY 1 2 3 4 5 HA

GEAR / SET UP

TARGET AREA

♂

♀

AMMUNITION

ACTIVITY & SIGHTINGS

TYPES OF FLORA

ADDITIONAL NOTES

DATE

TIME

LOCATION

WEATHER CONDITIONS

HUNTING TYPE

CO-HUNTERS

TERRAIN LEVEL

EASY 1 2 3 4 5 HARD

GEAR / SET UP

TARGET AREA

♂

♀

AMMUNITION

ACTIVITY & SIGHTINGS

TYPES OF FLORA

ADDITIONAL NOTES

DATE

TIME

LOCATION

WEATHER CONDITIONS

☀️ ⛅ 🌧️ ⛈️ ❄️

☐ ☐ ☐ ☐ ☐

HUNTING TYPE

CO-HUNTERS

TERRAIN LEVEL

	1	2	3	4	5	
EASY	○	○	○	○	○	HARD

GEAR / SET UP

AMMUNITION

TARGET AREA

♂ ☐

♀ ☐

ACTIVITY & SIGHTINGS

TYPES OF FLORA

ADDITIONAL NOTES

DATE

TIME

LOCATION

WEATHER CONDITIONS

HUNTING TYPE

CO-HUNTERS

TERRAIN LEVEL

1   2   3   4   5

EASY   HARD

GEAR / SET UP

AMMUNITION

TARGET AREA

♂

♀

ACTIVITY & SIGHTINGS

TYPES OF FLORA

ADDITIONAL NOTES

DATE

TIME

LOCATION

WEATHER CONDITIONS

HUNTING TYPE

CO-HUNTERS

TERRAIN LEVEL

1　　2　　3　　4　　5

EASY　　　　　　　　　　　HAR

GEAR / SET UP

TARGET AREA

♂
☐

♀
☐

AMMUNITION

ACTIVITY & SIGHTINGS

TYPES OF FLORA

ADDITIONAL NOTES

DATE

TIME

LOCATION

WEATHER CONDITIONS

HUNTING TYPE

CO-HUNTERS

TERRAIN LEVEL

1　2　3　4　5

EASY　　　　　　　HARD

GEAR / SET UP

AMMUNITION

TARGET AREA

♂

♀

ACTIVITY & SIGHTINGS

TYPES OF FLORA

ADDITIONAL NOTES

📅 DATE	**WEATHER CONDITIONS**
🕐 TIME	🌡 ___ ☀ ⛅ 🌧 ⛈ ❄
📍 LOCATION	🚩 ___ ☐ ☐ ☐ ☐ ☐

HUNTING TYPE

🎯 HUNTING TYPE

🧑‍🌾 CO-HUNTERS

TERRAIN LEVEL

🌳 EASY — 1 ⭕ — 2 ⭕ — 3 ⭕ — 4 ⭕ — 5 ⭕ HA

GEAR / SET UP

AMMUNITION

ACTIVITY & SIGHTINGS

TARGET AREA

♂ ☐

♀ ☐

TYPES OF FLORA

ADDITIONAL NOTES

DATE

TIME

LOCATION

WEATHER CONDITIONS

HUNTING TYPE

CO-HUNTERS

TERRAIN LEVEL

EASY 1 2 3 4 5 HARD

GEAR / SET UP

AMMUNITION

TARGET AREA

♂

♀

ACTIVITY & SIGHTINGS

TYPES OF FLORA

ADDITIONAL NOTES

DATE

TIME

LOCATION

HUNTING TYPE

CO-HUNTERS

WEATHER CONDITIONS

TERRAIN LEVEL

1   2   3   4   5

EASY   HARD

GEAR / SET UP

AMMUNITION

TARGET AREA

♂
☐

♀
☐

ACTIVITY & SIGHTINGS

TYPES OF FLORA

ADDITIONAL NOTES

DATE

TIME

LOCATION

WEATHER CONDITIONS

HUNTING TYPE

CO-HUNTERS

TERRAIN LEVEL

1 2 3 4 5

EASY   HARD

GEAR / SET UP

TARGET AREA

♂

♀

AMMUNITION

ACTIVITY & SIGHTINGS

TYPES OF FLORA

ADDITIONAL NOTES

DATE

TIME

LOCATION

WEATHER CONDITIONS

HUNTING TYPE

CO-HUNTERS

TERRAIN LEVEL

EASY   1   2   3   4   5   HARD

GEAR / SET UP

TARGET AREA

♂
☐

♀
☐

AMMUNITION

ACTIVITY & SIGHTINGS

TYPES OF FLORA

ADDITIONAL NOTES

DATE

TIME

LOCATION

WEATHER CONDITIONS

HUNTING TYPE

CO-HUNTERS

TERRAIN LEVEL

1   2   3   4   5

EASY ○ ○ ○ ○ ○ HARD

GEAR / SET UP

AMMUNITION

TARGET AREA

♂
□

♀
□

ACTIVITY & SIGHTINGS

TYPES OF FLORA

ADDITIONAL NOTES

DATE

TIME

LOCATION

WEATHER CONDITIONS

HUNTING TYPE

CO-HUNTERS

TERRAIN LEVEL

EASY 1 2 3 4 5 HA

GEAR / SET UP

TARGET AREA

♂

♀

AMMUNITION

ACTIVITY & SIGHTINGS

TYPES OF FLORA

ADDITIONAL NOTES

DATE

TIME

LOCATION

WEATHER CONDITIONS

HUNTING TYPE

CO-HUNTERS

TERRAIN LEVEL

EASY 1 2 3 4 5 HARD

GEAR / SET UP

AMMUNITION

TARGET AREA

♂

♀

ACTIVITY & SIGHTINGS

TYPES OF FLORA

ADDITIONAL NOTES

DATE

TIME

LOCATION

WEATHER CONDITIONS

🌡 ____ ☀ ⛅ 🌧 ⛈ ❄

🚩 ____ ☐ ☐ ☐ ☐ ☐

HUNTING TYPE

CO-HUNTERS

TERRAIN LEVEL

EASY	1	2	3	4	5	HARD
	○	○	○	○	○	

GEAR / SET UP

AMMUNITION

TARGET AREA

♂ ☐

♀ ☐

ACTIVITY & SIGHTINGS

TYPES OF FLORA

ADDITIONAL NOTES

DATE

TIME

LOCATION

WEATHER CONDITIONS

HUNTING TYPE

CO-HUNTERS

TERRAIN LEVEL

1   2   3   4   5

EASY   HARD

GEAR / SET UP

AMMUNITION

TARGET AREA

♂

♀

ACTIVITY & SIGHTINGS

TYPES OF FLORA

ADDITIONAL NOTES

DATE

TIME

LOCATION

WEATHER CONDITIONS

HUNTING TYPE

CO-HUNTERS

TERRAIN LEVEL

EASY 1 2 3 4 5 HARD

GEAR / SET UP

TARGET AREA

♂
☐

♀
☐

AMMUNITION

ACTIVITY & SIGHTINGS

TYPES OF FLORA

ADDITIONAL NOTES

DATE

TIME

LOCATION

WEATHER CONDITIONS

HUNTING TYPE

CO-HUNTERS

TERRAIN LEVEL

EASY 1   2   3   4   5 HARD

GEAR / SET UP

TARGET AREA

♂
☐

♀
☐

AMMUNITION

ACTIVITY & SIGHTINGS

TYPES OF FLORA

ADDITIONAL NOTES

DATE

TIME

LOCATION

WEATHER CONDITIONS

🌡 ___ ☀ ⛅ 🌧 ⛈ ❄

🎏 ___ ☐ ☐ ☐ ☐ ☐

HUNTING TYPE

CO-HUNTERS

TERRAIN LEVEL

	1	2	3	4	5	
EASY	◯	◯	◯	◯	◯	HA

GEAR / SET UP

AMMUNITION

TARGET AREA

♂ ☐

♀ ☐

ACTIVITY & SIGHTINGS

TYPES OF FLORA

ADDITIONAL NOTES

DATE

TIME

LOCATION

HUNTING TYPE

CO-HUNTERS

WEATHER CONDITIONS

TERRAIN LEVEL

1   2   3   4   5

EASY   HARD

GEAR / SET UP

AMMUNITION

TARGET AREA

♂

♀

ACTIVITY & SIGHTINGS

TYPES OF FLORA

ADDITIONAL NOTES

📅 **DATE**	**WEATHER CONDITIONS**
🕐 **TIME**	🌡️ —— ☀️ ⛅ 🌧️ ⛈️ ❄️
📍 **LOCATION**	🚩 —— ☐ ☐ ☐ ☐ ☐

| ⊕ **HUNTING TYPE** | **TERRAIN LEVEL** |
| 👨‍🌾 **CO-HUNTERS** | |

EASY 1 2 3 4 5 HARD

GEAR / SET UP

TARGET AREA

♂ ☐

♀ ☐

AMMUNITION

ACTIVITY & SIGHTINGS

TYPES OF FLORA

ADDITIONAL NOTES

DATE

TIME

LOCATION

WEATHER CONDITIONS

🌡 ———   ☀ ⛅ 🌧 ⛈ ❄
🚩 ———   ☐   ☐   ☐   ☐   ☐

HUNTING TYPE

CO-HUNTERS

TERRAIN LEVEL

EASY 1 ———— 2 ———— 3 ———— 4 ———— 5 HARD
⭕ ———— ⭕ ———— ⭕ ———— ⭕ ———— ⭕

GEAR / SET UP

AMMUNITION

TARGET AREA

♂
☐

♀
☐

ACTIVITY & SIGHTINGS

TYPES OF FLORA

ADDITIONAL NOTES

DATE

TIME

LOCATION

WEATHER CONDITIONS

HUNTING TYPE

CO-HUNTERS

TERRAIN LEVEL

1   2   3   4   5

EASY   HAR

GEAR / SET UP

TARGET AREA

♂

♀

AMMUNITION

ACTIVITY & SIGHTINGS

TYPES OF FLORA

ADDITIONAL NOTES

DATE

TIME

LOCATION

WEATHER CONDITIONS

HUNTING TYPE

CO-HUNTERS

TERRAIN LEVEL

EASY 1 2 3 4 5 HARD

GEAR / SET UP

AMMUNITION

TARGET AREA

♂

♀

ACTIVITY & SIGHTINGS

TYPES OF FLORA

ADDITIONAL NOTES

DATE

TIME

LOCATION

WEATHER CONDITIONS

🌡 —

💨 —

☀ ⛅ 🌧 ⛈ ❄

☐ ☐ ☐ ☐ ☐

HUNTING TYPE

CO-HUNTERS

TERRAIN LEVEL

🌳 1 2 3 4 5
EASY ◯ ◯ ◯ ◯ ◯ HA

GEAR / SET UP

AMMUNITION

TARGET AREA

♂
☐

♀
☐

ACTIVITY & SIGHTINGS

TYPES OF FLORA

ADDITIONAL NOTES

DATE

TIME

LOCATION

HUNTING TYPE

CO-HUNTERS

WEATHER CONDITIONS

TERRAIN LEVEL

EASY   1   2   3   4   5   HARD

GEAR / SET UP

AMMUNITION

TARGET AREA

♂

♀

ACTIVITY & SIGHTINGS

TYPES OF FLORA

ADDITIONAL NOTES

DATE

TIME

LOCATION

HUNTING TYPE

CO-HUNTERS

WEATHER CONDITIONS

TERRAIN LEVEL

EASY 1 2 3 4 5 HARD

GEAR / SET UP

AMMUNITION

TARGET AREA

♂
☐

♀
☐

ACTIVITY & SIGHTINGS

TYPES OF FLORA

ADDITIONAL NOTES

DATE

TIME

LOCATION

HUNTING TYPE

CO-HUNTERS

WEATHER CONDITIONS

TERRAIN LEVEL

1   2   3   4   5

EASY   HARD

GEAR / SET UP

AMMUNITION

TARGET AREA

♂

♀

ACTIVITY & SIGHTINGS

TYPES OF FLORA

ADDITIONAL NOTES

Copyright ©
All rights reserved. No part of this publication may be reproduced, distributed,
or transmitted in any form or by any means, including photocopying, recording,
or other electronic or mechanical methods, without the prior written permission
of the publisher, except in the case of brief quotations embodied in critical reviews
and certain other noncommercial uses permitted by copyright law.

Made in the USA
Las Vegas, NV
12 December 2023

82611929R00059